FROM FILMATION'S GHOSTBUSTERS

(c) 1986 ™

GHOSTBU[illegible]S™

Annual 1987

CONTENTS

Published in Great Britain by World International Publishing Limited, An Egmont Company, P.O. Box 111, Egmont House, Great Ducie Street, Manchester M60 3BL.

Printed in Italy.

SBN 7235 6788 3

The Hungry Trucker's Revenge

Meatball Mulligan, the fattest trucker in the state of Kentucky, had been on the road for three days. Now he was only a couple of hours from home and he picked up the CB set in his cab to warn his wife of his impending arrival. "Okay, honey," he said into the microphone, "your big buffalo is homeward bound on this liquorice stick so make sure my plate's piled high with pie. And a side of that fatback bacon. And half a dozen eggs. And a gallon of your coffee and a tub full of fried potatoes."

Meatball Mulligan loved Mrs Mulligan's cooking. Whenever he was away from home he would dream about it. Now, as he drove his truck into a tunnel in the Blue Ridge Mountains, he was thinking about a pile of pancakes two feet high. With a big bowl of syrup. And a big jug of cream. And a bunch of bananas chopped up on top. And then, maybe, a watermelon to follow.

Meatball was so busy dreaming about his dinner that at first he did not notice how long the tunnel was. However, by the time that his daydream had reached a twenty-fifth course of baked prune Alaska on a bed of rice pudding and walnuts, he realised that there was something wrong. There was no other traffic in the tunnel and the white line in the middle of the road had begun to wriggle like a worm. Strange, scary faces with glowing eyes and grinning mouths and fat, stone tongues that squirmed like slugs began to appear on either side of the truck and the walls of the tunnel echoed with ghostly, screeching peals of laughter.

Suddenly the truck emerged from the tunnel and stopped of its own accord. Meatball peered curiously around him. The truck had stopped in a huge, vaulted chamber surrounded by high windows and old cobwebbed wooden doors. Somewhere a clock struck midnight. Oh boy! thought Meatball to himself as a set of crocodile teeth floated past him, snapping at the empty air, this place is WEIRD! Maybe it was some kind of new fangled funfair, he thought to himself as skeletons and different coloured ghosts ran howling between the different doors. And if it is a funfair, he thought, as he climbed down from his cab, then there had to be an ice-cream stall and a burger stand nearby.

"Say, buddy," he yelled out as a figure approached him. "You with the metal head. You know where I can get a cheeseburger? And a milk shake? And some ice-cream? And maybe . . ."

Suddenly the horned figure reached out a claw and a bolt of ghostly blue light shot out and lifted the fattest trucker in Kentucky ten feet up into the air. Sharp spikes came up

from the ground below him and Meatball looked down and began to shake with fright.

"Be silent, you great blubbering ball of blancmange!" shrieked the figure. "Do you not realise that you are in the presence of Prime Evil, master of misrule? That I reign supreme in the spirit world?"

"If you say so, goodbuddy," said Meatball, looking nervously down at the spikes.

"Good," said Prime Evil as the spikes disappeared and the trucker floated down to the ground like a balloon. As his toes touched the ground a strange, sparkling mist floated from Prime Evil's cape and disappeared into Meatball's eyes. His eyes began to spin around like coloured discs and when they stopped there was a strange, vacant stare in them. "You must understand that you no longer work for the Ace Trucking Company. From now on, Meatball, you work for the forces of darkness. Do you understand me?"

"I understand and will obey, oh mighty one," said Meatball Mulligan.

"Excellent," said Prime Evil, placing a claw on the shoulder of the hypnotised trucker. "Your first task will be to drive back down the Scareway to ancient Egypt and bring me ten stones from the head of the Sphinx. My servants are already there, waiting to load them. After that I shall need you to bring me the tails of ten thousand newts, eleven tons of radioactive dust from the planet Bloop, the bones of a billion bats, the eggs of twelve dinosaurs, the bark from a hundred haunted trees, three hundred skulls – any old skulls will do – and seven teeth from the giant terrapin of Grok."

At 13 Canterbury Street, the air was rent by a sudden, blood-curdling shriek of surprise. Tracy had been feeding the ghoulfish and it had bitten his finger. As the strongest Ghostbusting gorilla in the world leapt around the office, trying to shake the ghoulfish's teeth loose from his fingertip, he disturbed Belfry, who had been hanging upside down from the grandfather clock letting its ticking and tocking lull him to sleep. The little bat began to flutter angrily around the room, shrieking at Tracy. Skelevision, who had been showing them a news item from England about the mysterious disappearance of the roof from the Albert Hall, became irritated at the disturbance and turned up a channel of white noise, full blast. Jake was just about to put his hands over his ears when he heard the Ansabone's call signal begin to bleep and the spectral telephone snarled, "You want some spare ribs, then try asking a skeleton! This is Ghost Command not the Chinese takeaway!"

"Hello. Ghostbusters. Can we help you?" said Jake, snatching up the receiver before the talking bone could do any more harm.

"Glad to find an apple out in skipland with his flappers on," said a voice. "I been pumping dust ever since I hit the solar system. I'm inward bound from the dark dimensions on the flip flop, kangarooing newts' tails and looking for a chip shop. I been hammer toed to Bloop and Grok without so much as a cup of mud. I've blown the doors off comets and shooting stars on the spaceway superslab and I've ridden the liquorice stick back to dinosaur times and I've still not been down for the count. I've seen red giants, black holes, and white dwarves but I aint seen a diner since South Carolina and that was so far back now I don't know WHEN it was. Goodbuddy, you are listening to one tired and hungry sunbeam, so if you know of a place I can get a loaf and ..."

Jake was just about to reach for the alien

language decoder unit when another voice interrupted the first and the young Ghostbuster's nose began to twitch ominously – the second voice belonged to the most gruesome, ghastly ghost of them all, Prime Evil. Putting his hand over the mouthpiece, Jake signalled the other Ghostbusters to silence. Belfry stopped in mid screech, Skelevision turned down his sound, and Tracy, with the ghoulfish's teeth still clamped around the end of his finger, gritted his teeth, screwed up his eyes, and swallowed the shriek of pain he had been about to give.

"Well, my moronic Meatball," hissed the Ghostbusters' arch enemy, "have you got the newts' tails I need for my potion?"

"That's a big ten ten, my horrid badbuddy. I got you a fat daddyfull and we should be peeper to peeper by noon. Then maybe I could go and get myself a plate of ..."

"Be careful, mortal. I have warned you before about how you address me," hissed Prime Evil as Jake listened silently. "I tolerate you only because I need your truck to transport the ingredients of my potion for me. Otherwise I would have already fed you to one of my pet werewolves. Do I make myself clear?"

"As clear as a glass of cream soda, most mighty and magnificent one," Jake heard the trucker say. "Please forgive my momentary impertinence, but my stomach has been empty for so long that my head is beginning to spin. In fact, I was just saying to this Peter rabbit ..."

"What!" exclaimed Prime Evil angrily. "You mean to tell me you have been talking to someone on your stupid toy!"

"Sure have, most powerful and perfect one," said Meatball Mulligan cheerfully. "Some dude with the handle Goatbuster, or Ghostcustard, or something like that. Why don't you ask him yourself? He's still got his ears on."

"Ghostbusters!" exclaimed Prime Evil angrily. "Kong! Are you there! Are you listening?"

Jake held his breath. Tracy and Belfry did likewise. The Ghostbusters' office was silent. And then Eddie came in and asked who had ordered the bacon, lettuce and tomato sandwich.

"Did you say sandwich, goodbuddy?" asked Meatball Mulligan excitedly before Prime Evil gave a shriek of wild, demented rage and filled the airwaves with a shrill, deafening scream.

"Forget the sandwiches, Eddie," said Jake, putting down the Ansabone, "we've got Ghostbusting to do. Prime Evil's cooking up a potion and, by the sound of it, it's got to be a big one. He's captured a truck driver to move the ingredients for him. We better go and find him."

"Oh sure," said the Ansabone. "I get a call that could come from anywhere in time and space and you say 'let's go find him'. It should be simple."

"The truck driver mentioned white dwarfs and red giants," said Jake. "That can only mean one thing."

"Yeah," said Eddie, "a circus."

"No, Eddie," said Jake. "Red giants and white dwarfs are stars. And he mentioned the fact that he'd been to Bloop and Grok. They're both planets. And there was something about the solar system. He's somewhere in space and . . ."

Jake broke off as he saw Tracy, finally free of the ghoulfish, pushing a lawnmower up and down the office. He wore a white coat and had a stethoscope around his neck.

"Tracy's right!" exclaimed Jake. "Let's go see Doctor Mower."

There was the usual flurry of captive ghosts whizzing and wailing round the Ghost Command Offices as the Ghostbusters linked arms and yelled "Let's go, Ghostbusters!" and then they had dropped down to the garage and the waiting Ghost Buggy. Wondering aloud whether he would have been happier as a taxi, G.B. puttered out into Canterbury Street.

Doctor Mower was an astronomer. He ran a huge radio telescope on a hill close to the town. When the Ghostbusters got there he told them that there had been strange shooting stars in the vicinity of Hawaiian Islands. As the pleasant, grey-haired scientist led them around the foot of the giant telescope, Jake asked him what had been strange about the shooting stars.

"Well, young Kong," said Doctor Mower, adjusting his glasses and scratching his head, "I know it sounds ridiculous, but some of the shooting stars were shaped just like a sixteen wheel truck!"

Immediately the Ghostbusters climbed into G.B. and set off for the Pacific Ocean. As they approached the Hawaiian Islands, Eddie got a reading on the spectre detector and following its signal they were soon swooping down on Hawaii, the largest island in the chain.

However, as the Ghost Buggy emerged from the thick clouds, the Ghostbusters were greeted by a most extraordinary sight. There, clinging to the side of Mauna Loa, the huge smoking volcano, was the giant shape of Hauntquarters. And placed across the smoking top of the volcano, like a giant Chinese cooking pan, was the upturned roof of the Albert Hall. And into it, Prime Evil and his skeleton slaves were tipping the ingredients of his potion from the back of Meatball Mulligan's truck, which was covered in space dust, cobwebs, meteor scars, and ectoplasmic ooze from its fifty billion mile journey through space and time. In front of the truck, Scared Stiff stood guard over the exhausted, sleeping form of Meatball Mulligan.

"That's right, my bony beauties," crooned Prime Evil to his skeletons as they shoved two more blocks from the ancient Egyptian Sphinx into the mixture, "two more lumps should make it sweet enough, and now the potion is ready. One cupful can make a person's dreams real. Two cups can make them bigger than real. Three can make them gigantic. And I have gallons and gallons of the stuff! Imagine it, Scared Stiff! Once we have drunk our fill of this mixture, every last horrible, tiny monster that enters our imagination shall become real! And not only real but gigantic! Then the people of Earth shall cringe in terror before me and I shall have all the power I want!"

As Jake listened to Prime Evil's mad boasts a smile came to his face. "I know how we can bust these clowns," he said, pulling the dematerialiser from his ghostpack. "Let's go and get Meatball!"

At Jake's command, Tracy sent the Ghost Buggy into a steep dive. The car's seats sprang up on springs. Eddie pulled a large magnet from his ghostpack and Scared Stiff was pulled up into the air by it. As his metal bolts clunked against the magnet, Jake blipped him with the dematerialiser then, with the help of the other two Ghostbusters, hauled the sleeping shape of Meatball Mulligan into the Ghost Buggy.

"Kong!" exclaimed Prime Evil in surprise as the Ghost Buggy swooped down over the top of the bubbling, treacly, lukewarm mixture. "So you and your friends think you can interfere once more! Well this time you are too late!"

"That's what you think, Prime Awful!" yelled Jake. "Let's bust this clown!"

With that the Ghostbusters pushed the still sleeping Meatball out of the Ghost Buggy and down into Prime Evil's potion. There was a great, bubbling splash as

Kentucky's fattest trucker hit the surface, took a couple of swallows, smiled, and then slowly sank. Immediately the whole mixture began to seethe and bubble and then, up from out of the upturned roof of the Albert Hall, came an unstoppable torrent of gargantuan cheeseburgers, baked potatoes, chips, pancakes, apples, oranges, and cream cakes. Coleslaw, ice-cream and trifle ran down the mountainside in oozing rivers and as it threatened to engulf Hauntquarters, Prime Evil retreated up the Scareway and disappeared to another dimension. Meanwhile, sardines, cherry pies, sausage rolls and cucumber sandwiches the size of houses continued to bubble up from the potion. Suddenly the potion was still. And then, slowly, looking like a creature from a deep dark swamp, the figure of Meatball Mulligan appeared once more.

"Thanks, goodbuddies," said the trucker as G.B. lowered a rope and winched him up and then dropped him down on the ground beside his truck.

"Thank you, Meatball," yelled Jake. "Once we've neutralised this potion and got the roof back on the Albert Hall maybe we could give you a lift home."

"Not just yet, friends," yelled Meatball, looking round wide-eyed at the huge mountains of food. "I got some serious eating to do before I go."

Have you ever wanted to be a Ghostbuster? Have you dreamed of blipping felonious phantoms back across the dark dimensions with the dematerialiser? Do you think you've got what it takes to trap a ghost in the electrospectral suppressor unit? Have you ever wanted to punch holes in an evil force field with a particle accelerator beam?

You have? Well remember, Ghostbusting can be a dangerous business. You can get bitten by ghoulfish, bumped on the head by bones, have your senses scrambled by a sonic scream, or find some ghost with a ghastly sense of humour has just shoved an ectoplasm pie in your face. And that's all before you've even left the Ghost Command Offices at 13 Canterbury Street!

But if you're still keen to try, then you should get to know what kind of ghosts you're up against. First, take a look at these dusty documents drawn from the deep dark depths of the Dead Letter File. They're filed, when you can find them, under H, for they come from the file marked . . .

Hauntquarters Horrible Henchghosts

In his plan to subject every living creature to his power, Prime Evil uses ghosts and spectres from every zone and era of the dimensional timescape. Some, however, have particular powers which make them more important to him. We have listed these, along with identifying photographs and, when we could think of any, suggestions on how they might be defeated.

Signed and dated, Eddie Spenser senior

Jake Kong senior

Little Eddie

Jake Kong junior

X Tracy's Mark

APPARITIA
A witch. Magic: Black. She wanders the spirit world with a glistening ball in tow. A couple of magic words and a wave of her long fingered hands can conjure up all manner of apparition from her crystal ball (eg. 17.6.72 Skeleton gun fighter with ten gallon hat or 12.3.85 fire breathing dragon). The more you believe in Apparitia's apparitions, the more real they become.

BRAT-a-RAT
Prime Evil's tattletale pet. He is a cross between a bat, a rat, a ghoul, a gremlin, a creepy caterpillar and a monstrous maggot. Prime Evil uses him to spy, often on his other ghosts.

FANGSTER
From the Hominus Lupus Luna species of spectre. When the moon is full this werewolf can travel to any era from his lair in the future. His weapon belt is equipped with all manner of grisly gadget, and his large, heavy plasteelium boots enable him to launch himself head or feet first at anything unwise enough to stand in his way. When doing so he resembles a hairy missile with fangs.

FIB FACE

This gruesome ghost-goblin possesses two faces, both of them horrible. He is completely incapable of telling the truth. One face will say one thing, then his head will spin round and the other face will say the exact opposite. He uses this tactic to confuse and bewilder his enemies. However, by asking him the right questions, it's possible to turn Fib Face's magic on himself, for once you can get the two faces arguing his head spins round faster and faster as each face tries to win the argument.

FLOATZART

An evil and extremely odd looking conductor whose secret weapon is a magic baton capable of producing hypnotic, trance like music which will put all mortal creatures who hear it under his power. His chief weakness is his temperament, for when the mad maestro of musical malice is ignored he is likely to pound his baton in a furious fit of temper, causing the most carefully laid of Prime Evil's plans to collapse in chaos and confusion.

The Haunted Pipes of Invermuckly Glen

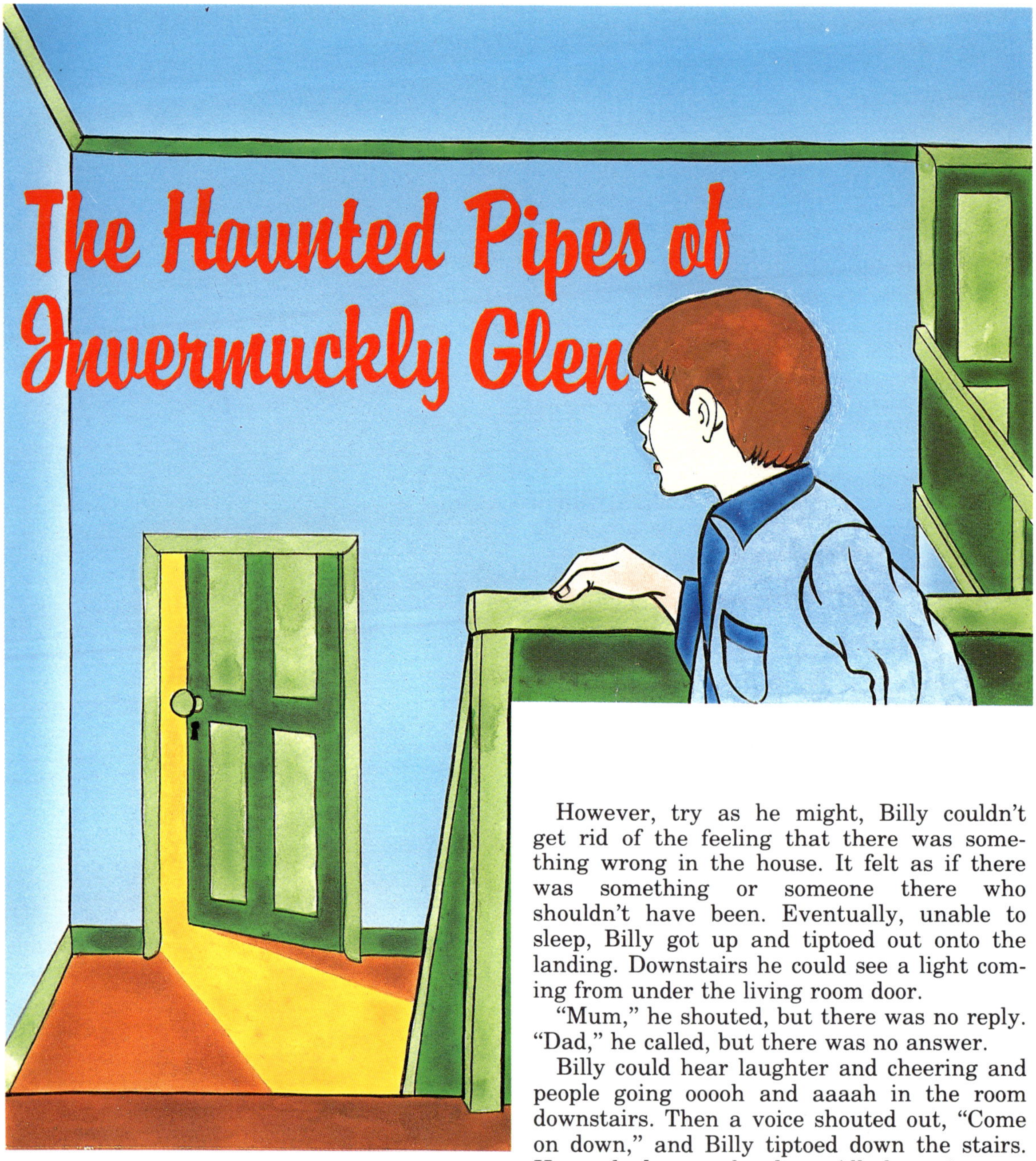

One still, hot summer's night, Billy McDiggle dreamed that his mum and dad had been turned into wax. The dream was so horrible, and so frightening, and so real, that Billy was relieved when he woke up from it. However, no sooner had he done so than he saw two glowing, round yellow eyes in a pale white face staring out of the darkness at him. Billy sat up in bed with a start, then realised that the eyes belonged to the family's fluffy white Persian cat, Fergus. Billy smiled as Fergus jumped down from his bed and padded silently round the open door. Then he tried to get back to sleep again.

However, try as he might, Billy couldn't get rid of the feeling that there was something wrong in the house. It felt as if there was something or someone there who shouldn't have been. Eventually, unable to sleep, Billy got up and tiptoed out onto the landing. Downstairs he could see a light coming from under the living room door.

"Mum," he shouted, but there was no reply. "Dad," he called, but there was no answer.

Billy could hear laughter and cheering and people going ooooh and aaaah in the room downstairs. Then a voice shouted out, "Come on down," and Billy tiptoed down the stairs. He pushed open the door. All the noise was coming from the television set. His parents were watching "The Price is Nice". Billy peered over the back of the sofa where his mum and dad usually sat and gasped in horror. There, sitting perfectly still, was a bright green, ghostly spectre!

Terrified, Billy ran out of the room into the dark hallway. He didn't know what to do or where to go and his heart was beating faster than it had ever beaten before in his life. Then, suddenly, he heard a terrible, terrified miaow from Fergus. The poor cat seemed to be trapped somewhere and Billy hurried up the stairs to see what was the matter.

Once he reached the upstairs landing he heard the cat miaow again. The sound came from the attic, and Billy looked up the flight of narrow stairs that led up there. The trapdoor at the top was normally closed but tonight it was open, and from beyond it came a glowing, ghostly light and the sound of a strange, hissing voice arguing and laughing quietly. Billy wished his mum or his dad were there to tell him what to do. But they weren't. Billy realised that if Fergus was in trouble, he'd have to rescue him himself. Slowly, treading softly so that the floorboards beneath his feet wouldn't creak, Billy tiptoed up the stairs and peered into the attic.

There, amongst the bottomless chairs, rusty bedsteads, old calendars, mothballed clothes, broken toys, and dusty suitcases, standing over an open tin trunk, were three ghosts. One was a beautiful woman with a strange, silver ball floating in the air beside her head. Another was a wicked looking goblin with two faces. And the third was a hunter with a pith helmet, khaki shorts, and a horrible, cruel smile. On his back there was a crossbow, and in his ghostly, transparent hands something long-haired, white, and furry was lying perfectly still.

"Fergus!" exclaimed Billy angrily, and forgetting his fear he ran across the attic to rescue his cat from the three ghosts. However, as he did so, the woman waved her fingers around the silver ball and from it appeared a shining silver needle that flew around the attic, trailing a bright silver thread around everything in the room. Billy tripped over the thread where it was stretched between a headless tailor's dummy and an old, broken grandfather clock. The headless dummy fell down with a crash in front of him and the clock struck midnight. Before he could get to his feet there was a booming, grating sound, like huge stones being rubbed against one another, and a strange glowing doorway appeared in the middle of the attic.

"We've got what we came here for," exclaimed the ghost in the helmet, holding the motionless furry form tight in his hands. Then he disappeared through the doorway as it began to close. The goblin with two faces followed him, then the lady and the silver ball. And then, last of all, when the entrance was no more than the narrowest crack of light in the centre of the attic, the silver needle flew through it. Then there was a thud, like heavy doors make when they are closing, the silver thread snapped, and the attic was silent. In the moonlight that streamed through a cracked, dusty skylight in the sloping roof, Billy watched the silver thread float to the floor and disappear. He thought about his mum, his dad and his cat, and he wondered what to do. Then, all of a sudden, he felt a hand on his shoulder. He turned around, and there, staring down at him, was his father.

"What are you doing up here in your pyjamas, Billy?" his father asked him.

"Dad! You're all right!" gasped Billy.

"Of course I am," said his father, smiling. "Your mother and I must have dozed off while we were watching the television. I was woken by a noise from up here and . . ."

"But you and mum weren't there, and there were three ghosts here, and they took Fergus with them and . . ."

"Sssshhhhh, Billy," said his father gently as he led his son out of the attic and closed the door. "You're beginning to sound like your great uncle Angus. Everybody knows there's no such thing as ghosts. You just had a bad dream."

"But Dad," protested Billy as he climbed back into bed, "it was a dream at first and then it was real. I saw them. There was a goblin with two heads, and a hunter with a big moustache, and . . ."

"Sssshhhhh," said his father again as Billy lay down. "You'll have forgotten all about it in the morning."

But when morning came, Billy McDiggle hadn't forgotten any of it. The ghosts were still there in his memory, as clear as day, and when he could find no sign of Fergus anywhere, he decided to go and see his great uncle Angus.

At 13 Canterbury Street, the Ghostbusters were trying to recapture a harmless but particularly mischievous ghost called Gregory who had escaped from an electrospectral ghost storage tank that morning. Tracy had tried to lure Gregory out of hiding by leaving an ectoplasm pie on the desk for him but before he could put the pie down, Gregory had come cackling out of the Dead Letter File, snatched the pie from the gorilla's hands, and shoved it in his face. As Tracy wiped a mixture of custard, cranberries, and ectoplasmic ooze from his eyes, Belfry's high pitched shriek of laughter brought part of the ceiling down on their heads. Now, covered from head to toe in white plaster, the Ghostbusters were trying to figure out where Gregory had hidden.

"He's probably already gone," said Eddie.

"I don't think so," said Jake, "he'll find it hard to get out since we've had the doors ghost-proofed and the spectral glazing put on the windows." Then he looked round the Ghost Command Offices and shouted, "Are you still here, Gregory?" There was a single, loud knock in reply. Eddie grinned at Jake and put a thumb in the air. "Is that you, Gregory?" asked Jake. Once more there was a single, loud knocking noise. "All right," said Jake. "Give one knock for yes, two for no. Do you understand, Gregory?" There were two knocks. "Just quit fooling around and tell us where you are," said Jake impatiently. This time there was a furious flurry of rapping and Tracy banged a hand against his forehead and opened the door. Standing there was a small boy and an old man in a kilt. The old man still held a wooden walking cane raised in the air.

"It's nae wonder you dinna answer," he said looking at Jake and Eddie in alarm. "There have been big changes since I was last here. You two used to be Ghostbusters but now it seems you're ghosts."

"We're not ghosts," said Eddie.

"Ye cannae fool me, laddie," said the old man, shaking his head, "you've neither of you aged a day since I saw you in forty nine, and you're both sitting there all grinning and ghostly white and your big mate the monkey is dripping all over with that ectothing-ummyblob stuff. Of course you're ghosts!"

"No, we're not," said Jake, grinning and dusting the white plaster from his uniform. "The reason we don't look any older is that the Ghostbusters you saw in forty nine were our fathers."

"Well, tickle my tartan socks!" exclaimed the man. "Then perhaps I better introduce myself. My name's Angus McDiggle. Your daddies helped me sort out a wee problem with a set of haunted bagpipes back in forty nine. Now my great grand-nephew Billy has had his cat stolen by ghosts."

As Billy told the Ghostbusters about the ghosts he had seen in his attic, Jake's face became serious. "It sounds like Apparitia, Fib Face, and The Haunter have been up to their magic tricks again," he said. "Let's go and see what they wanted with your cat."

"You mean you'll help us find Fergus!" exclaimed Billy happily.

"Sure we will, Billy," said Jake, and the three Ghostbusters linked arms and yelled, "Let's go, Ghostbusters!"

In the usual chaotic, cacophonous swirl of ghosts, gremlins and spectres that followed, Gregory the ghost slipped into Tracy's ghostpack.

Gregory remained hidden in the ghost-pack until the Ghostbusters reached Billy's house. Then, as they made their way up to the attic, he slipped quietly through a crack in the floorboards, chuckling silently to himself.

"They were over there," said Billy, pointing across the attic to the tin trunk. The Ghostbusters made their way across to the trunk. As they got closer they heard a strange, scratching noise from inside it. Eddie held the dematerialiser at the ready and Jake slowly lifted the lid. No sooner was it open than out sprang Fergus the cat. Billy ran across and picked up the fat, white cat and began to stroke it.

"If they didn't come for the cat," said Eddie,

"then what did they come for?"

"Aye, laddies," said Angus McDiggle, looking down into the empty trunk, "it's just as I feared. The curse of the McDiggles is at work again. It was the sporran of Drunken Duncan McDiggle that they were after."

"Who was he?" asked Eddie.

"He was my cousin," said Angus, "the laird of Invermuckly Glen. When I left for America, cousin Duncan gave me a wee black box and his sporran. In the sporran was the key to the box. He told me that the box contained the haunted bagpipes of Invermuckly Glen. Of course I didna believe him and once I got here I took a wee peek." Angus McDiggle shook his head. "It was a horrible sight to behold. If it hadna been for your daddies, those pipes would be walking the world today!"

"Then what happened to them?" asked Jake.

"After we captured them, I put them back in their box and buried it," said Angus. "I left the key and a map of where I'd buried the pipes in the sporran. And I left the sporran in the tin trunk."

"And now Prime Evil and his pals have got the map!" exclaimed Jake. "Can you remember where you buried them, Angus?"

Angus rubbed his beard, scratched his head, and then nodded. Moments later, the three Ghostbusters, along with Angus and Billy McDiggle, were racing across the countryside in the Ghost Buggy. Suddenly the air was filled with a hideous, ghostly wailing sound.

"The pipes!" gasped Angus. "We're too late! Look!"

The Ghostbusters looked. Down below them, in a clearing in some trees on a river bank, Prime Evil and Scared Stiff stood beside a hole in the ground. On the edge of the hole was a black box with the lid open. And striding through the trees like some hideous giant spider in a tartan waistcoat were the haunted bagpipes of Invermuckly Glen.

"This time you are too late, Kong!" laughed Prime Evil as the Ghostbusters leapt from G.B. "Take them prisoner, pipes!"

Under Prime Evil's command, the giant pipes turned towards Jake and his friends. With every horrible note that came from them, ghosts and ghouls, spirits and spectres were floating up into the air. Slowly the pipes marched onward toward the Ghostbusters. Eddie covered his eyes. Jake reached for the dematerialiser and began to blip the ghosts back to their own dimensions as they attacked, but still the pipes came on.

"I know how we can bust these clowns!" exclaimed Jake suddenly. "We've got to get those pipes into the water!"

Slowly, the Ghostbusters and the two McDiggles retreated from the advancing pipes. Then, when they reached the banks of the river, the three Ghostbusters brought lassoes from their ghostpacks and flung them over the haunted pipes of Invermuckly Glen. The pipes reared in the air and gave a wild shriek, kicking furiously as the Ghostbusters dragged them out into the water. The air was thick with ghosts howling about the Ghostbusters' heads and then the pipes began to fill with water and their skirling sound began to bubble and wheeze. Then, with a final, defeated squeak, they fell silent, the ghosts all disappeared, and with an enormous splash, the giant pipes keeled over on their side and lay still. Prime Evil gave a roar of frustrated rage and then he and Scared Stiff disappeared up the Scareway. Meanwhile, in the shallow water of the river, the haunted pipes of Invermuckly Glen had shrunk to their normal size.

"I think that maybe we better keep these pipes at Ghost Command, Angus," said Jake, as he put the waterlogged pipes back in the black box and turned the key.

"Aye laddie," said Angus McDiggle, shaking his head with relief. "I think that mebbe you're right."

Later that day, when Billy's father came home from work, Billy tried to tell him all about how the Ghostbusters had found Fergus for him and how they'd captured the haunted pipes of Invermuckly Glen. Billy's father smiled as he took the coffee percolator off the stove and opened a cupboard to get himself a cup.

"I've told you before, Billy," he said, "there's no such thing as gh ..." There, sitting on the shelf between two jelly moulds and cackling furiously to himself, was Gregory the ghost.

Hauntquarters

Horrible Hench Ghosts

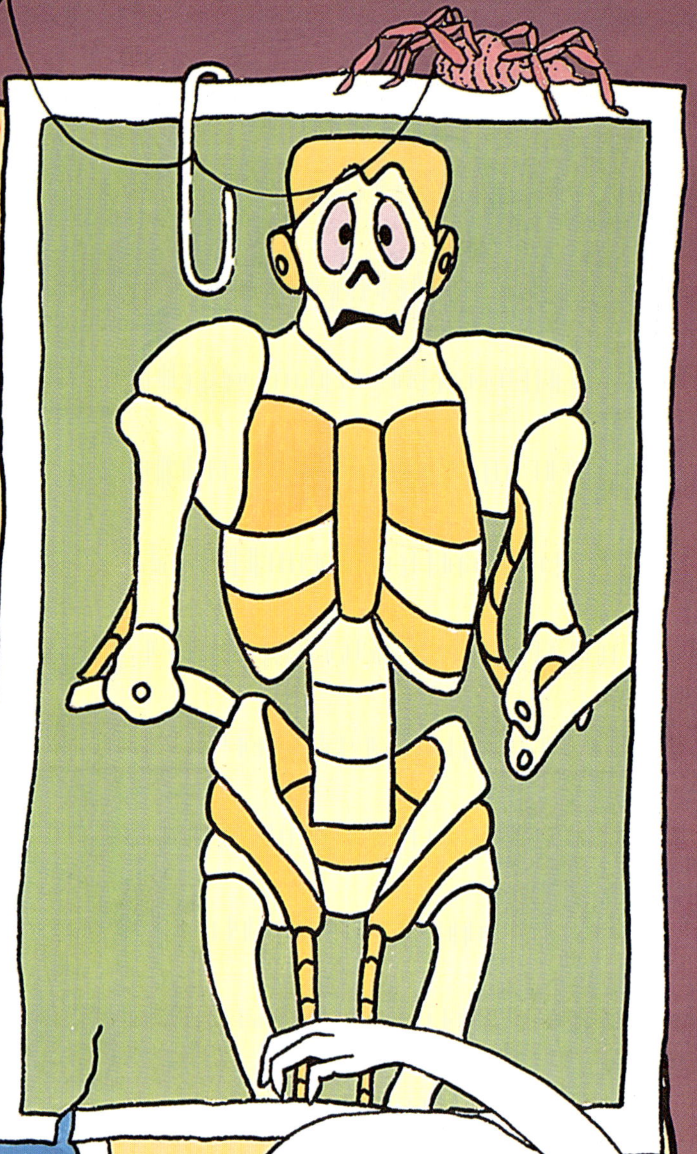

SCARED STIFF

A snivelling robot skeleton from the future, Scared Stiff has enough nuts and bolts and rivets to open up an ironmongers. He is a master of high tech sabotage and has a mysterious power over things mechanical. If you've got a ghost in one of your machines, most likely it was Scared Stiff that put it there. Scared Stiff is probably the most harmless of all Prime Evil's ghosts, usually more scared than he is scary. It's easy enough to find him when he's hiding because he can't control his bones and bolts when he starts shaking and they clatter and clank and fly off all over the place.

THE HAUNTER

He is the ghost of an English big game hunter, easily recognisable by his dastardly chortle. If he doesn't chortle you can still recognise him by his pith helmet, khaki shorts, and magic monocle. His helmet can change size and he uses it as a means of transportation as he stalks through time with his spirit crossbow, forever searching for new ghosts to capture for Prime Evil.

MYSTERIA

A witch spirit. She can transform herself into a shadowy, fluctuating mist that can trip up or tie up her enemies. When she appears in a more visible, human form she is exceptionally vain, a trait which you can sometimes use to defeat her.

LONG JOHN SCARECHROME

A future version of a marauding, plank-walking pirate. He has a chrome eyepatch, a hook for a hand, and a spring-loaded metal peg leg. He has sensitive radar antennae in his pirate's hat and haunts the spaceways of the cosmos in a transparent rocket with skull and crossbones on the side, performing his crazed acts of piracy.

SIR TRANCEALOT
A former Knight of the Round Table, Sir Trancealot haunts the heavens dressed in dark forbidding armour, perched on his hollow eyed horse, **FIGHTMARE**. Fightmare is easily recognised by his helmet and distinctive moustache. Sir Trancealot got his name from his deadly weapon, the Trance Lance – a long, pointed jousting spear that causes his victims to lapse into a deep and undisturbable sleep. Like most of Prime Evil's cronies, Sir Trancealot is only brave when he has might on his side. When the chips are down and the fat's in the fire, however, he can be as easily frightened as Scared Stiff.

SOMEWHERE BEYOND SPACE AND TIME, IN A HIDDEN CORNER OF THE MULTIVERSE, STANDS A BROODING, NAMELESS FORTRESS . . .
ENTER THE DRAGON SLAYER
. . . WHERE DEEP IN THE DEEPEST DUNGEONS, SOME OF THE MOST EVIL APPARITIONS IN SPIRITDOM SERVE OUT THEIR TIME BEHIND SPECTRAL BARS . . .
WHOOAAHHA
THE FELONIOUS PHANTOMS ARE WATCHED OVER BY YUM-YUM, A BENEVOLENT SPIRIT WITH NO WEAKNESSES . . .
. . . EXCEPT ONE!
BLIP
SLURP! DREADED WHEAT WITH SPOOK-ETTI SAUCE! MY FAVOURITE!
YUM-YUM DIGS IN, UNAWARE OF THE SECRET, SPRITELY ADDITIVE CONTAINED IN THE SAUCE. AN INGENIOUS INGREDIENT . . .
YUM-YUM-YUMMY!

. . . COOKED UP BY THE DIABOLICAL VILLAIN, PRIME EVIL!
HA-HAAA! NOW YOU HAVE EATEN THE SAUCE YOU ARE IN MY POWER!
THE SINISTER SPECTRE WASTES NO TIME . . .
RELEASE THE PRISONERS! FREE THEM ALL!
YES, MASTER.
BEEUYUY
. . . AND EVIL RUNS AMOK!
GO, MINIONS AND HENCH GHOSTS! CREATE HAVOC ON PLANET EARTH!
BEEHUHUHH!
AND SO IT WAS THAT IN ENGLAND, AT THE TIME OF KING ARTHUR . . .
JUST ONE MORE DAB OF HEMLOCK IN MY POTION . . .
GULP! I MUST HAVE USED TOO MUCH SALT, FORSOOTH!
AND, AT 13 CANTERBURY STREET, IN THE PRESENT TIME . . .
I WARNED YOU NOT TO TAKE TRACY TO THE FOOTBALL GAME.
COME ON, JAKE, HOW WAS I TO KNOW HE'D EAT THE BALL!

SUDDENLY . . .
WHAT DO YOU MEAN YOU AIN'T GOT NO NUMBER? PUT YOUR MONEY IN, YOU CHEAPSKATE!
1 2 3 4 5 6 7 8 9
JAKE INTERVENES . . .
HELLO? . . . THE MERLIN? . . . YOU SAY SOME GHOSTS ARE TRYING TO MAKE KING ARTHUR GO MAD? WE'RE ON OUR WAY!
SO . . .
LET'S GO, GHOSTBUSTERS!
OWWLLLLL!
EEEK!
AND . . .
HEYYY! YOU GOTTA CUT DOWN ON THE BANANAS, TRACY!
BRUSH UP ON YOUR MANNERS, GUYS, WE'RE OFF TO SEE KING ARTHUR!

SOON . . .
LOOK! IT'S KING ARTHUR – JOUSTING!
YEAH, BUT THAT'S NOT THE BLACK KNIGHT
. . . IT'S SIR TRANCEALOT!
LOOK OUT, SIRE!
BLOING
HOLD ON, FELLERS!
QUICK, TRACY – THE DEMATERIALISER!
FIZZZBLAT!
FOR ONCE, EVERYTHING GOES RIGHT . . .
YOU'RE HISTORY, FANCY-LANCE!
WELL, ALMOST EVERYTHING . . .
IT'S NO USE, TRANCEALOT MUST HAVE SCORED A HIT.
HEY! GHOST BUGGY! WAKE UP!
LATER . . .
I MANAGED TO TRAP THE GHOSTS IN THIS MAGIC JAR.
YEAH, LET'S HOPE IT'S NOT . . .
NICE WORK, MERLIN, BUT THE SPECTRE DETECTOR SAYS THERE'S ONE MORE STILL FREE.

–IT IS! PRIME EVIL!
GOT IT IN ONE, GOODY-GOODY! YOU HAVE PROVIDED AN EXCELLENT DIVERSION FOR MY MAIN PLAN . . .
GAZKS
. . . TO STEAL MERLIN'S WAND AND DESTROY THE DIMENSIONAL FABRIC THAT SEPARATES GHOSTS FROM HUMANS!
Y-Y-YOU WON'T GET AWAY WITH IT. TRACY, HAND ME THE FIEND FRYER!
GLOOP!
GLEEP
I SAID THE FIEND FRYER! NOT AN OLD GAS OVEN!
GLEEP?
ZZZ
YOU PUNY INCOMPETENTS! SEE HOW MERLIN'S MAGIC PULVERISES YOUR PATHETIC OFFERING!
CHOOOO
HE'S TURNED IT INTO DUST!
UH . . . UH . . .
METAL DUST! A . . . A . . . A . . .

CHOOOO
HA! MERE DUST CANNOT HURT ME! PREPARE TO MEET YOUR DOOM!
BUT AS THE LOATHSOME SPIRIT-LEADER ACTIVATES THE WAND, THE METAL DUST SETTLES ON HIS SPECTRAL FORM . . .
UNH! WHAT'S HAPPENING?
ZZZZZ
. . . CREATING AN ELECTRO MAGNETIC SHIELD THAT LOCKS THE POWER INSIDE!
THE FOUL FIEND IS FORCED TO FLEE . . .
WHOOSH
HE'S HISTORY!
FOR NOW, ANYWAY. AND AT LEAST HE DIDN'T GET THE WAND!
WE MUST CELEBRATE WITH A FEAST!
AND . . .
YOU'RE GOING TO NEED A GUARD ON THE GHOULS IN THE GLASS.
YES, PERHAPS THE KING COULD HELP ME THERE . . .
LATER . . .
THE GHOST OF THAT DRAGON YOU SLEW YESTERDAY MAKES AN EXCELLENT JAILER, SIRE.
SURE DOES. HEY, PASS THE WATER JUG, JAKE.
SORRY EDDIE, I CAN'T REACH IT FROM HERE.
I'LL HAVE TO GET ANOTHER JUG OR CHANGE THE SHAPE OF THIS TABLE.

The Curse of Big Caesar's Pyramid

Even by the awful standards of Gangstonia, it was a very rough night indeed. Raindrops the size of golf balls plopped down from the sky, and the chill wind screeched like phantom fingernails on some ghostly blackboard, giving jerky, unnatural life to the twisted branches of the mis-shapen trees, and underscoring the grim, unearthly whispering of their leaves with the hideous mindless howling of the forces of the night. As a distant clock signalled the arrival of the witching hour, Johnny pulled his talking hat, Homburg low across his brow, thrust his freezing hands deeper into the pockets of his thin cotton jacket, stuck out his chin and carried on along the lonely, country road. He knew only too well that if he hadn't insulted his robot bicycle by drawing attention to the large red spot on its plasteelium fairings he could have been at home asleep in bed like any normal Gangstonian and not trudging through the bitter cold towards a parental castigation that would make twenty years at the oars of a Roman galley seem like a weekend trip on the love boat.

And then the hairs on his neck started rising, his eyes bulged, and he had the sudden overwhelming conviction that someone was beating a big bass drum inside his chest. Ahead of him, in the moaning, buffeting darkness, the grotesquely distorted malformation of a headless, three-armed monster with two glowing eyes in the middle of its chest, reared up from behind a hedge and swayed menacingly above him. As he tried to will his legs to spring into action, and one of the flickering luminescent orbs began moving, circling the other in a monstrous parody of nature, sudden thunder boomed, lightning cracked, and in the fleeting flash of the electric thunderbolt, Johnny saw that the scene that had set the icy hands of terror clutching at his heart was nothing more than two fireflies inside a knot hole in a dead tree trunk.

"Huh!" said Johnny, unconvincingly. "I ain't afraid of no ghost!"

"Baloney, shortcake!" replied Homburg, perched precariously on the top of Johnny's upraised hair. "When your mother washes the sheets you hide in the coalshed."

"I like counting the lumps, that's all," explained Johnny defensively.

Homburg laughed cruelly. "You're just a scaredy cat!" he sneered. "If you had any guts you'd get out of this rain and shack up for the night in Big Caesar's Pyramid!"

"But ... but ... it's haunted!" Johnny gulped. "And it's cursed!"

"So? You ain't afraid of no ghost, remember?"

Johnny felt his upper lip go soft. If only he'd settled for a set of whistling knee-pads instead of that stupid hat. Everybody knew that Big Caesar's Pyramid was no place to spend the night. After all, hadn't the great Big Caesar himself disappeared forever in there when he used it as a hideout? The pyramid, with its miles and miles of unexplored passageways and secret tunnels had been there for as long as anyone on Gangstonia could remember, but ever since Big Caesar vanished there when he broke out of jail after stealing the world's last remaining fragment of blutonium superputty, it had been known as Big Caesar's Pyramid. Neither Big Caesar nor the blutonium had ever been seen since.

"All right, you has-been head warmer," said Johnny rashly, regretting the words as they tumbled from his mouth. "I will!"

Johnny crept across the fields to Big Caesar's Pyramid. Although the cavernous structure stretched many thousands of feet under the ground, the top was little bigger than a house; a squat, four-sided building covered with mysterious carvings and signs.

"How do we get in here?" asked Johnny. Homburg shifted uneasily on his head.

"Maybe it wasn't such a good idea after all," he whispered. "Maybe..." Homburg fell silent as one of the carvings in the nearest rectangular panel started creaking and suddenly the outline of the werewolf's head on it began to shift and change, and as Johnny and Homburg watched in mounting terror, the horrible face of Prime Evil appeared, a ghostly arm lashed out, and Johnny was dragged inside Big Caesar's Pyramid while Homburg flew off and rolled, bouncing and blubbering with fear, across the fields to the road.

By the time Johnny had got control of his senses he had been hauled into a secret chamber inside Big Caesar's Pyramid that already held the gruesome figures of Prime Evil, Fangster, Mysteria and Scared Stiff. He half-closed his eyes and nibbled the ends of his fingers as he stood squinting around the ghost filled room. First, Prime Evil began

humming loudly, then Mysteria began singing in a weird, high-pitched voice. Fangster made grizzly, growling noises and Scared Stiff tapped out a lively rhythm on his head. When the monstrous music reached a creepy crescendo there was a flash of light and suddenly, in the middle of the room, the ghost of Big Caesar appeared, a spectral cigar clamped firmly between his ghoulish, blubbery lips!

"At last!" crowed Prime Evil, his hideous voice booming in the cavernous chamber. "Now we can begin my plan! And this insignificant earthlet can watch as the entire cosmos is overrun with ghosts!"

As the evil, despicable despot's eerie laughter echoed in the half-light, Johnny summoned up all his courage, then turned and ran for his life.

Inside Ghost Command, Eddie and Tracy were heading a football to each other across the desk while Jake wiped tomato sauce off the report he was trying to write up for Jessica Wray's latest item on the Phantom News Network. Eddie ducked down to loop the ball over Jake's head, and as the super-strong gorilla rose to meet it, Belfry let out a shriek of disgust at the fact that the egg in his egg and pickle sandwich was uncooked and Tracy jerked his head upward, catching the ball with the back of his head. It cannoned up into the air, knocking Belfry from his perch and scattering the offending sandwich, ricocheted off the wall and slammed down onto the Skelevision control bone. The weird, swirling colours on Skelevision's screen spun faster, the screen flickered and hissed and the face of a very distraught talking hat appeared, a hanky held to its glistening eye.

"You've got to help me!" it sobbed, "Somebody, anybody, please. It's my master, Johnny – I think he's been kidnapped by ghosts!"

Jake adjusted the tuner and the Ghostbusters listened attentively as Homburg told the sad tale. Then they raced to the transportation section, linked arms, yelled, "Let's go, Ghostbusters!" and after the usual whizzing, howling whirlwind of spectres, djinn and imps, ghouls and flibbertigibbets, they landed ready for action in the Ghost Buggy at the bottom of the trapdoor.

"I knew I should have got a job as a fire engine," joked Ghost Buggy, as Tracy bounced up and down in the driver's seat. Then the old jalopy's engine squeaked into life, the rickety doors creaked open, and the Ghostbusters puttered out to meet a new chilling challenge!

Later, as Tracy looked for an opening into Big Caesar's Pyramid, Jake and Eddie tried to decipher the weird markings contained in one of the panels on the ancient artefact's walls.

"I don't want to alarm you or anything," said Eddie, pushing some buttons on his solar powered tape of Cyphers Of Unknown Cultures, "but if I read these signs right, they say 'Death shall befall all who enter here'."

"It's probably just some old superstition," said Jake. "What do these markings in the next panel say?"

Eddie pressed a few more buttons and a worried gleam came into his eye. "They say that the pyramid was built as a kind of fort, to guard Gangstonia from some kind of overlap in the trans-dimensional flux. The builders called it the Twinning Zone."

"We'll soon find out why," observed Jake.

"It looks like Tracy's found a way in."

Jake was right. The world's strongest gorilla had managed to loosen one of the panels and was now lifting it up to reveal a phantasmagoric passageway, ringed with cobwebs. The three Ghostbusters stepped gingerly inside. The tunnel was lit by torches, burning on the wall. Jake picked one up and led the way, the flickering flames casting strange shadows on the walls. Tiny creatures scuttled around in the darkness. Ahead of them, a shiny suit of solid gold armour stood against the wall. The Ghostbusters were tiptoeing past when, without warning, the armour moved and a golden finger tapped Eddie on the shoulder. Before he could scream, the floor gave way and Eddie, Jake, Tracy and the armour tumbled down a secret passage and landed in a heap at the feet of Prime Evil!

"So, you decided to come and watch my moment of triumph!" crowed the gloating ghoul. "Here in the Twinning Zone, using Big Caesar's superputty to power my gyrotic oscillobox, I shall create millions of clones of my magnificent self so I can dispense with my minions and rule over eternity all on my own!"

"You've been taking the stupid pills again," Jake taunted bravely, as behind him the visor of the golden helmet lifted and Johnny's head appeared. "We're going to bust you clowns!"

"Oh yes?" mocked Prime Evil, pulling a lever on his oscillobox. "How?"

"Yeah, how?" asked Eddie nervously.

The box glowed and shook and tiny replicas of Prime Evil slid down the tube at the front, then slowly expanded to match the diabolical dictator's true size!

"I'm going to smash that box with my cosmic cane!" said Jake, stepping forward. "Tracy, hand it to me right now!"

"Gruh?" grunted Tracy, searching around in the bag as more and more Prime Evils appeared.

"The cane!" Jake urged. "Hurry!"

No sooner had he finished speaking than there was a howling of wind, the bag opened wide, and a real life hurricane came hurtling out! The whistling windstorm wobbled its way over to the box and danced around it, a furious tornado of twirling, tempestuous gale-force power that completely unbalanced the delicate gyros Prime Evil had used in his oscillobox. Suddenly, the clones began pouring out in horrible mismatching forms, some with two heads, some with gigantic feet, and some with no heads at all. Then the oscillobox exploded and the blutonium superputty power source sailed across the room into Jake's hands.

"I know how we can bust these clowns!" yelled Jake, as all the Prime Evil clones began arguing with themselves and the real one seethed with rage. Jake grabbed Scared Stiff while the simpering skeledroid cowered in a corner, then he and Eddie stretched the superputty between Tracy's upraised arms to make a giant cosmic catapult. Using Scared Stiff as the ammo, they pulled the putty back and released it, and the spectral slingshot sent the snivelling robot ghost smashing into his creepy cronies, bowling them all over and scattering them to the very edges of the Twinning Zone, where they glowed white, yellow, red, blue and green, and then vanished!

Back outside, while Johnny was reunited with Homburg, and Jake and Tracy prepared Ghost Buggy for the trip back home, Eddie stood with his finger to his mouth and a bemused expression on his face. "The thing I can't figure," he said slowly, "is how you knew the hurricane would wreck Prime Evil's fancy machine."

Jake looked up and winked. "I didn't!" he laughed. "But don't let anyone know. Keep it under your hat."

"No way, buster!" complained Homburg from his perch on Johnny's golden helmet. "I've got enough under here already!"

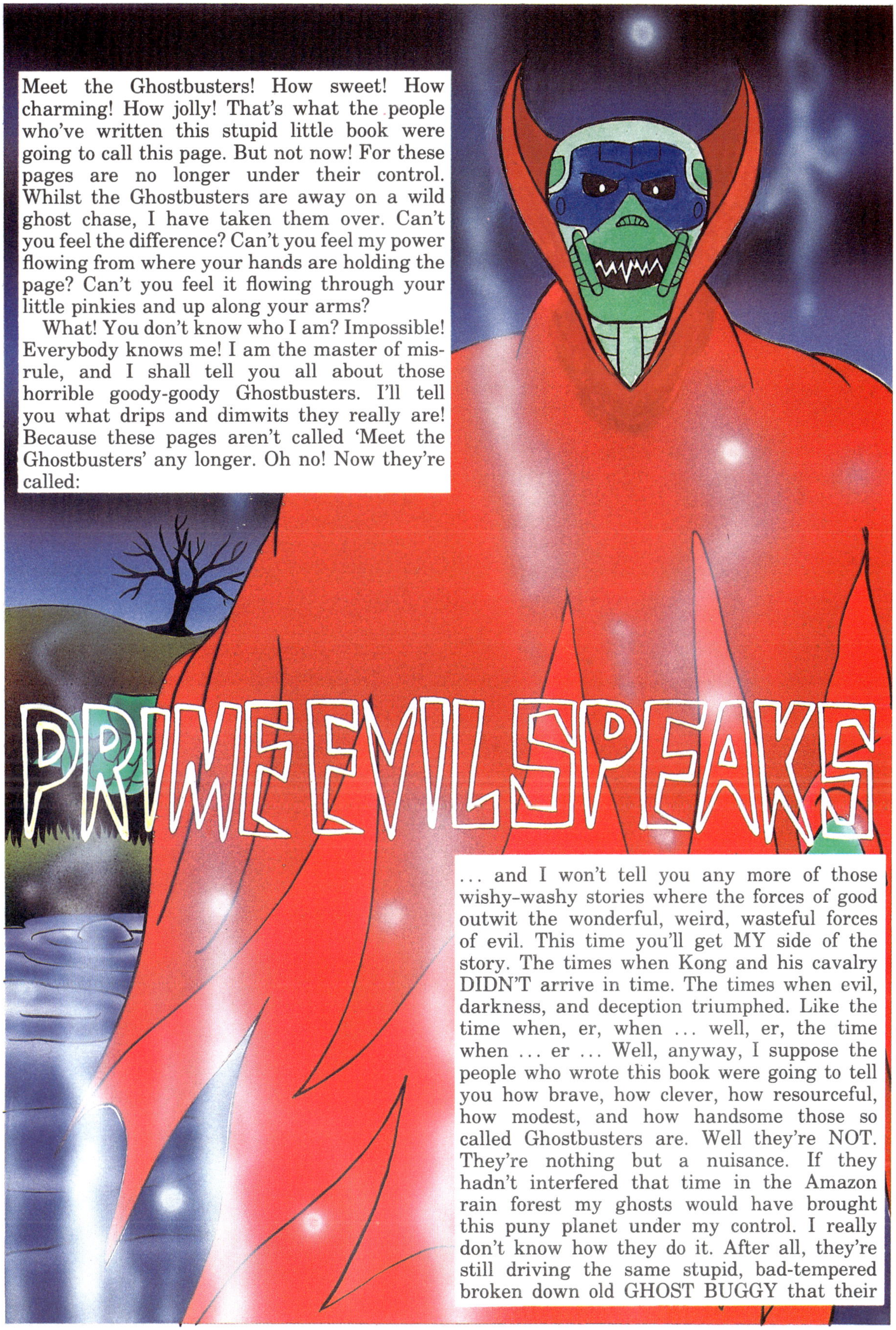

Meet the Ghostbusters! How sweet! How charming! How jolly! That's what the people who've written this stupid little book were going to call this page. But not now! For these pages are no longer under their control. Whilst the Ghostbusters are away on a wild ghost chase, I have taken them over. Can't you feel the difference? Can't you feel my power flowing from where your hands are holding the page? Can't you feel it flowing through your little pinkies and up along your arms?

What! You don't know who I am? Impossible! Everybody knows me! I am the master of misrule, and I shall tell you all about those horrible goody-goody Ghostbusters. I'll tell you what drips and dimwits they really are! Because these pages aren't called 'Meet the Ghostbusters' any longer. Oh no! Now they're called:

PRIME EVIL SPEAKS

... and I won't tell you any more of those wishy-washy stories where the forces of good outwit the wonderful, weird, wasteful forces of evil. This time you'll get MY side of the story. The times when Kong and his cavalry DIDN'T arrive in time. The times when evil, darkness, and deception triumphed. Like the time when, er, when ... well, er, the time when ... er ... Well, anyway, I suppose the people who wrote this book were going to tell you how brave, how clever, how resourceful, how modest, and how handsome those so called Ghostbusters are. Well they're NOT. They're nothing but a nuisance. If they hadn't interfered that time in the Amazon rain forest my ghosts would have brought this puny planet under my control. I really don't know how they do it. After all, they're still driving the same stupid, bad-tempered broken down old GHOST BUGGY that their

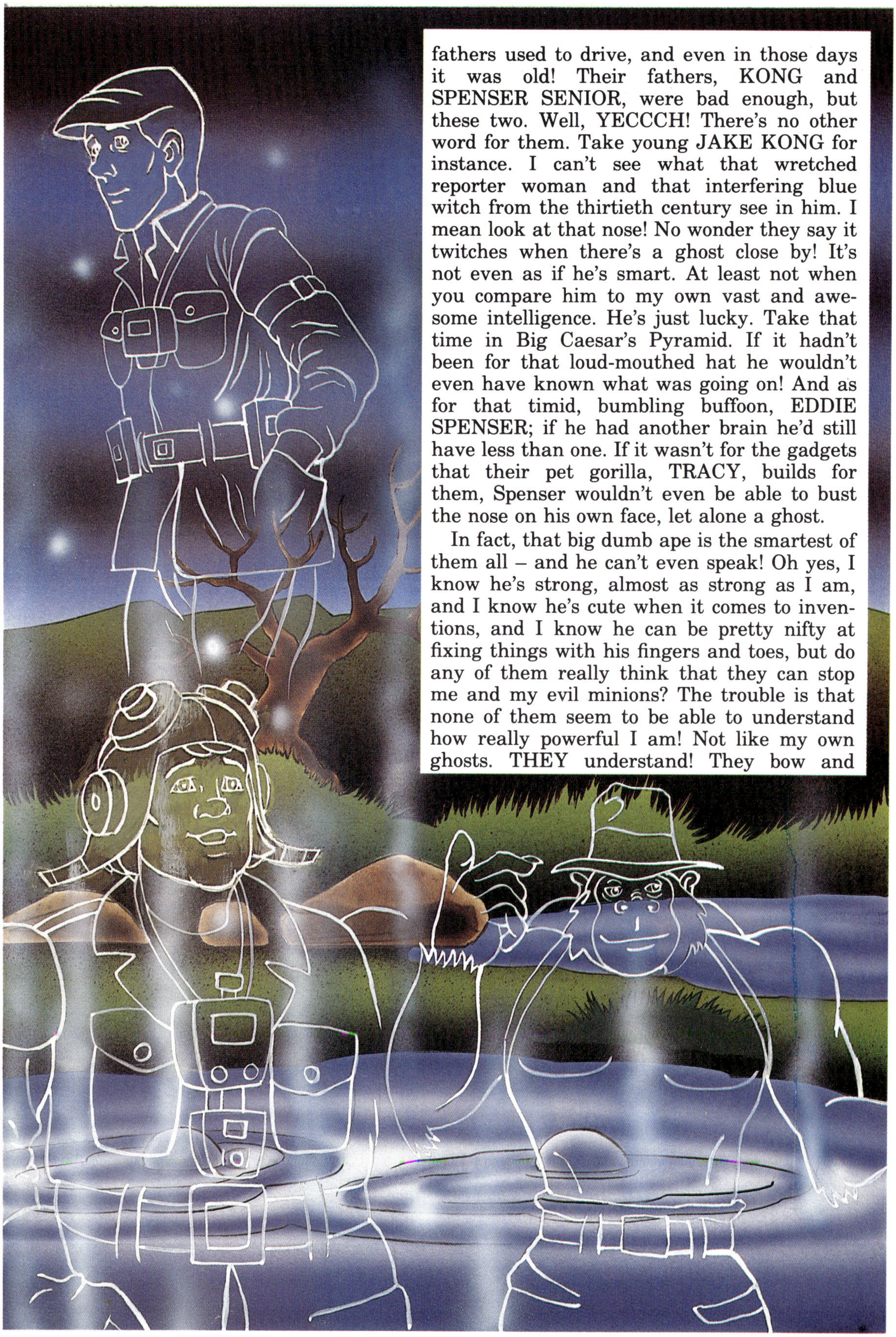

fathers used to drive, and even in those days it was old! Their fathers, KONG and SPENSER SENIOR, were bad enough, but these two. Well, YECCCH! There's no other word for them. Take young JAKE KONG for instance. I can't see what that wretched reporter woman and that interfering blue witch from the thirtieth century see in him. I mean look at that nose! No wonder they say it twitches when there's a ghost close by! It's not even as if he's smart. At least not when you compare him to my own vast and awesome intelligence. He's just lucky. Take that time in Big Caesar's Pyramid. If it hadn't been for that loud-mouthed hat he wouldn't even have known what was going on! And as for that timid, bumbling buffoon, EDDIE SPENSER; if he had another brain he'd still have less than one. If it wasn't for the gadgets that their pet gorilla, TRACY, builds for them, Spenser wouldn't even be able to bust the nose on his own face, let alone a ghost.

In fact, that big dumb ape is the smartest of them all – and he can't even speak! Oh yes, I know he's strong, almost as strong as I am, and I know he's cute when it comes to inventions, and I know he can be pretty nifty at fixing things with his fingers and toes, but do any of them really think that they can stop me and my evil minions? The trouble is that none of them seem to be able to understand how really powerful I am! Not like my own ghosts. THEY understand! They bow and

scrape before me. They obey my every word! They KNOW who's boss! Because they know what will happen to them, how horribly unpleasant I can make their existence if they don't do what they're told. But the Ghostbusters? Oh no! Not them! They're too stupid to see that they can't win! So they go on, all the time, interfering, confusing things, making trouble.

It's the same with their lady friends. Take that wrinkled, old goat MADAME WHY. Her gypsy wagon has been parked down the end of the pier since the days of Kong and Spenser Senior. She's supposed to be a fortune teller, but until her crystal ball was hooked up to a computer she couldn't even tell the time! And the blue one, the one they call FUTURA; if it wasn't for her magic amulet, the one that enables her to fly and disappear and change size and read minds, if it wasn't for that she'd have about as many magic powers as a garden gnome! And as for Jessica Wray, the reporter from the Phantom News Agency with the magic camera, they say that she's courageous and resourceful. Courageous and resourceful! I say she's just plain stupid. Imagine risking your life just for the sake of a story! Just so people can know the truth!

So there you have it! The so-called Ghostbusters are just a bunch of feeble, wishy-washy, incompetent nitwits. They're goofballs! No-good goody-goodies! I mean, if that's the best the forces of light can offer, how can they ever hope to triumph over the awesome, unseen forces of eternal dark?

YOU know they can't hope to win, don't you? Take an example! You're walking through the darkness on your own. The wind is blowing in the trees. There is no moon. An owl calls. And then, SUDDENLY, your torch stops working! All around you the darkness seems to be whispering, growling, howling, gurgling, giggling, hissing. YOU know there's something out there waiting for you, don't you? So why bother trying to be good? Why not just be bad? After all, being bad is so much more FUN!

Listen! If you promise to be really, really, really naughty, I'll tell you how to make a nuclear bomb from custard powder, old socks, and blutonium superputty. Then you'll be able to blow up the house next door! And everything else in the world! It's simple really, all you have to do is ... What was that noise?!?!?! Kong!!!!! What are you doing here? I thought ... What do you mean, THE WIZARD told you I was trying to take control of your book? No! Keep away from me with that, that THING! All I wanted were three or four miserable pages. You could have had the rest. Now I shall have to unleash all of my ... No! Don't touch me with the dematerialiser! I'm warning yaaAAAAAAAAAAAAAAAA-EEEEEEEEUUUUUURRRRRRRGGGGGG-GGGGGGGGHHHHHHHHHHHHHHH ... !

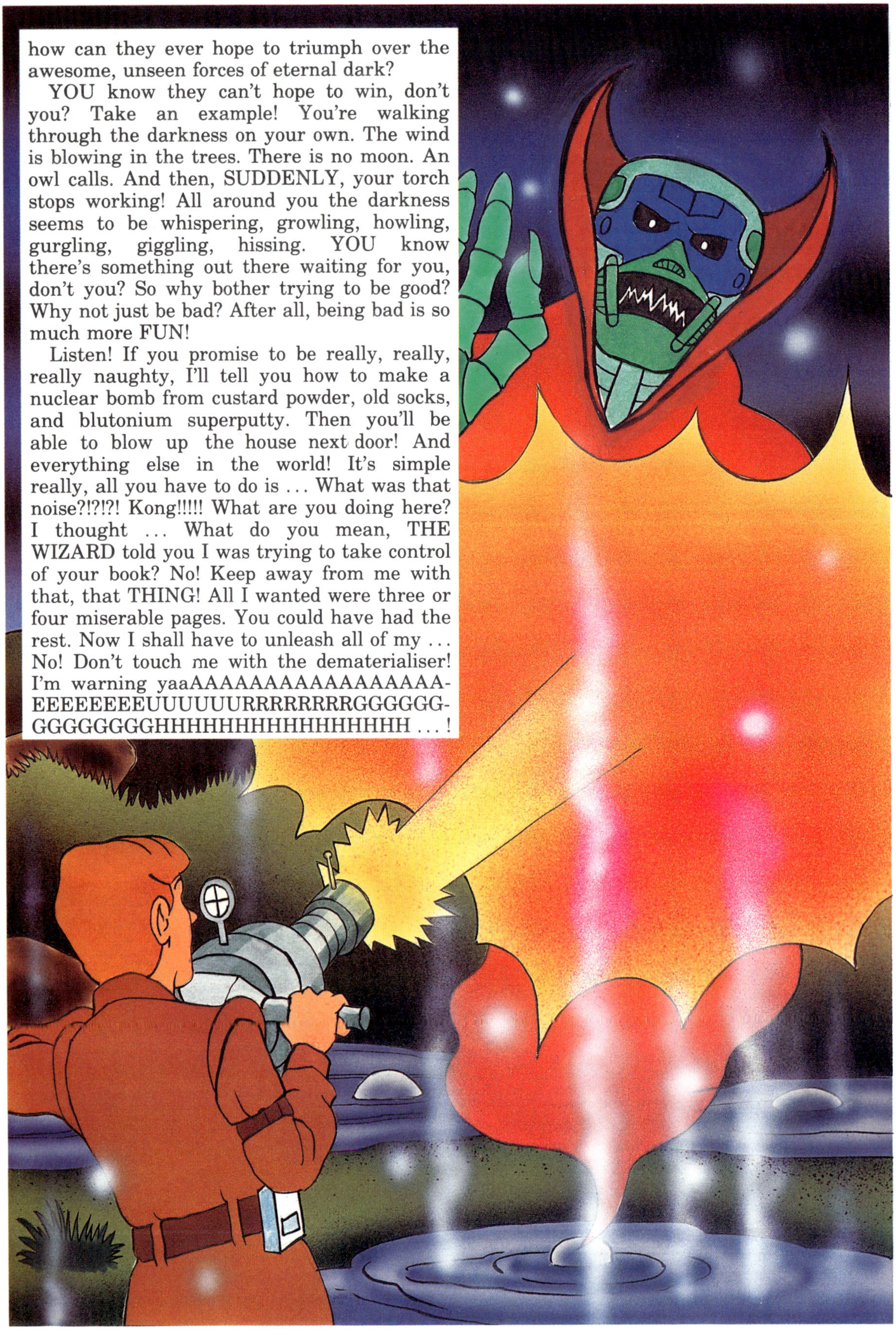

AMAZON ADVENTURE

Deep in the heart of the Amazonian rain forest, Abigail Rourke and Biff Brown, the stars of '*Amazon Adventure*', were tired, wet, and hungry. Cornelius Castrol, the movie's director, was telling them why they were going to have to shoot the scene again.

"Look, when the raft breaks up I want more splashing. It's splash, splash, splash and some screaming while you wait for the crocodiles to attack. By this time, the robots have almost caught up with you and start firing their lasers. You manage to get ashore with more splashing and more screaming. That's when you meet the dinosaurs – I want another big scream from you there, Abigail – but just when it seems that they're going to tear you to pieces, the spaceship arrives and takes you home to your own planet. Of course, you won't see the robots and the spaceship, we'll put them on the film when we get it back to the special effects lab, but act like you do anyway. You think you can do it?"

"Why not?" asked Abigail Rourke, wearily. "We've done it three times already."

"I know," said Cornelius Castrol impatiently, "but this time do it like you mean it. When you scream, scream with a little feeling. And Biff, when you punch the rubber crocodile you're just tapping it like you wanted to ask it the time. I want you to punch it as if it had just said something rude about your momma. Now, are you ready to go?"

"Sure, Cornelius," said Biff, "but maybe we should shoot this scene somewhere else."

"Oh, yeah?" said Cornelius Castrol, chomping a cigar down between his teeth and jutting his chin out aggressively. "Have you been listening to all that stuff about the wicked spirits of the Wariri?"

"Maybe we should listen to them, Cornelius," said Biff. "If the Wariri tribe say there are evil spirits here that shouldn't be disturbed, then maybe we shouldn't disturb them."

"Biff, if you think I'm going to let a load of primitive superstitions interfere with a movie when it's got my own bucks tied up in it, you must be crazy," said Cornelius Castrol. "Now, let's do the scene again."

Once more the two movie stars climbed onto the raft while Cornelius Castrol and the rest of the movie crew climbed into a motor launch. The cameras began to roll. The raft was swept over the rapids and Abigail screamed. The raft broke up and Abigail screamed again. Biff punched the rubber crocodiles as they were floated out towards him and then pointed to the robots that weren't there. They stumbled ashore through mud and overhanging trees with Cornelius

Castrol shouting encouragement from the launch through a megaphone. Then the dinosaurs appeared, great mechanical monsters that lumbered through the thick forest on tractor wheels.

Then, from the part of the forest where the spaceship was supposed to land, a group of natives armed with spears, blowpipes, bows and arrows and long, curved jungle knives came out of the trees. They were waving their arms in the air and shouting. Their faces were painted yellow and orange, their heads were decorated with the bright plumage of jungle birds. The leading dinosaur stopped, its head tilted back on giant hinges, and a hatch opened in its neck.

"Say! What's happening?" demanded the dinosaur driver, putting his head up out of the hatch. "This isn't in the scri . . ." The rest of what he was going to say was lost as he ducked down inside the hatchway and slammed the lid in terror. Immediately the dinosaur's head began to creak closed on its huge hinges and it reversed backwards crashing into the mechanical monster behind it. Both dinosaurs toppled over, smashing down into the mud and shallow water of the river, and their drivers scrambled out from the wreckage and swam as fast as they could to the launch, still filming off the shore.

Behind them, using the rubber crocodiles as stepping stones, came Biff Brown and Abigail Rourke. And Abigail was screaming louder than she had screamed all day, for there, coming through the trees towards them, was a ghost. And it was no ordinary ghost. It was fifteen feet high. And coloured purple. And fat, with long floppy ears like a spaniel's and what looked like a baseball cap on top of its tiny head.

As Cornelius Castrol watched, the enormous ghost creature leaned over and peered at the two mechanical dinosaurs. Then it began to chatter at them in a strange, clattering language that sounded like pennies being shaken inside a tin. Meanwhile, the Wariri indians had melted back into the trees as swiftly as they had come.

"All right," said Cornelius Castrol grimly, gazing back at the wreckage of his dinosaurs as the driver of the launch turned around and sped away from the weird, purple ghost, "if the Wariris and their evil spirits want trouble then they can have it. Get me those guys that do the ghostbusting stuff."

As soon as the Ghostbusters got the news from Skelevision that there was a ghost loose up the Amazon, they immediately dropped what they were doing. Belfry dropped the hazelnuts he was eating hung upside down on his perch. Tracy dropped the skin of the banana he was eating. Jake skidded on the hazelnuts, slipped on the banana skin and, as he sailed through the air, dropped the Encyclopaedia of Paranormal Happenings he was returning to the Dead Letter File. The sixteen hundred page book landed on the back of Eddie's head and he dropped the solar powered spanner with which he was adjusting the timing of the molecular vibrations on an electromagnetic matter modulator. Eddie reached into the machine to retrieve the spanner, trapped his fingers in an ionised particle duct and immediately got his molecules modulated.

"Yikes!" he said as he disappeared. Chairs started falling over all round the Ghost Command Offices as Eddie ran round in a panic crashing into them. Tracy reached into the refrigerator and pulled out some ice cubes.

"I think he's trying to tell you to keep cool," said Jake.

"Okay," said Eddie's disembodied voice. "Ask him when the effects will wear off."

Tracy grabbed a chainsaw and began to saw through a haunted grandfather clock that had been in Ghost Command since the days of Kong and Spenser Senior.

"In a short time," said Jake, halting the gorilla before he could do any more damage.

"Yeah, but how short?" demanded the invisible Eddie.

Jake looked at Tracy. Tracy looked thoughtful, scratched his head, and then shrugged. Then, linking their arms with their invisible partner's invisible elbows, the Ghostbusters yelled, "Let's go, Ghostbusters!" and all the spirits and spectres, ghosts and ghouls who had made their home at 13 Canterbury Street began to hoot and howl and then shoot through the air in shimmering, spectral whirls of colour as the Ghostbusters' ghostpacks dropped onto their backs and they tumbled down through their trapdoors and into the seats of the Ghost Buggy in the garage below.

"I don't suppose you guys ever thought of taking the subway to work," complained GB as Tracy landed with his fingers on the wheel and his toes on the pedals and Jake landed with an elbow in Eddie's invisible eye.

When GB finally arrived in the part of the jungle where the crew of '*Amazon Adventure*' had set up camp, they found it empty. As Jake and Eddie's empty uniforms crept between the tents and cabins with dematerialiser and vapour vacuum at the ready, Tracy scanned their surroundings with the super-

sensitive nozzle of the spectre detector. Jake asked him if there were any paranormal presences close by and the gorilla shook his head. As he did so, there was a rustling in the trees around them and they found themselves surrounded by Wariri warriors. And with the Wariris was Jessica Wray, ace reporter for the Phantom News Agency.

"Jessica, what are you doing here?" exclaimed Jake.

"Didn't you see my report on Phantom News?" asked Jessica. "I got the first flight down here as soon as I heard that *'Amazon Adventure'* had ghost trouble. When I got here the film crew were gone. I went into the forest to look for them. That's when I met Chief Charaba and the Wariris. He says he tried to warn Cornelius Castrol yesterday but he wouldn't listen. He's gone back to the haunted island to start filming again. Now the chief says that the evil spirits will destroy him and his film crew."

"Where did you learn to speak Wariri?" asked Jake, impressed.

"I didn't," said Jessica, "but Chief Charaba speaks English."

"What your friend Jessica says is true," said the Wariri in the brightest and tallest feathered head-dress. "The island has always been a place where ghosts walk, but recently our tribe's hunters say they have seen many, many spirits walking there. Cornelius Castrol and his film people are in great danger."

"All right," said Jake, "will you take us there?"

"I will take you," said Chief Charaba.

"Then let's go," said Jake.

Moments later, Jake, Tracy, Chief Charaba, Jessica Wray, and Eddie's empty Ghostbusting uniform were zooming over the forest and silver rivers in GB. When they saw the wreckage of Cornelius Castrol's mechanical dinosaurs they landed GB and made their way through the forest towards them. As they got closer they saw the huge purple ghost with the floppy ears and the baseball hat. The Ghostbusters tiptoed silently towards it, all of them bunched together behind Jake and the dematerialiser for safety. Suddenly, Jake heard a moaning sound, a soft popping noise, and felt something cold and clammy on his neck. The purple ghost looked up and saw them, gave a loud, rattling clatter of fright and ran off into the forest.

"S ... s ... sorry, Jake," said Eddie's voice behind him. "The febbers on the chief's head dress got up by dose and bade be sneeze."

"That ghost was even more scared than we were," said Jake thoughtfully, handing Eddie a hankie from his ghostpack.

"Of course he was frightened," cried a horribly familiar voice that hissed and echoed through the trees, "and with good reason! His name is Pibble and he is a ghost from the Galaxy of Gribble where everyone and everything is stupid. When he saw the two dinosaurs the foolish phantom thought they were robo-ghosts from his own galaxy and he went to play with them. The imbecile could have destroyed my whole plan. Now, when I catch him, I shall punish him. But first I shall deal with you meddlesome fools."

Suddenly from the trees all around them, winged ghost snakes of all different colours came whirling out and tied up the Ghostbusters and their friends in their spectral coils. Then the winged ghosts carried their captives back to a clearing deep in the trees. There, already held prisoner in wooden cages, were Cornelius Castrol, Abigail Rourke, Biff Brown, and the rest of the '*Amazon Adventure*' film crew. In the centre of the clearing were two huge, egg-shaped boulders and between them was a flat stone slab.

"My Bonetroller tells me that just here, between these boulders, lies the smallest of overlaps in the dimensional force fields," hissed Prime Evil, suddenly appearing in front of them. "It will only need the dimensional flux gates to open the tiniest fraction and your world will be overrun by my ghosts."

"And just how do you intend to open the gates, tin head?" demanded Jake as the Ghostbusters were disarmed and pushed into the cages.

"With a bit of bargaining, Kong," cackled Prime Evil. "As I throw you through the portal into the Ghost Dimension, my own ghosts shall pour through into your world and so shall begin my eternal reign of havoc, terror, and destruction."

"Listen, Cornelius," warned Abigail Rourke angrily when she heard Prime Evil speak. "Crocodiles, yes. Dinosaurs, yes. I don't even mind being tied up and put in a cage like this. But if you think I'M going to let

some weirdo push me into the Ghost Dimension without speaking to my agent first, then you better think again. I'm supposed to be the star of this picture."

As Abigail was protesting, Jake heard a whispering sound and looked down. There, shrunk to no more than an inch in size, was Futura, the beautiful blue-skinned sorceress from the thirty-first century.

"Futura!" whispered Jake. "What are you doing here?"

"When Pibble disappeared from the ghost zone in the Galaxy of Gribble I knew something was wrong. The ghosts there are too stupid to get away on their own. So I tracked him here."

"It's lucky for us you did," said Jake, and then began to smile. He snapped his fingers together and whispered, "I know how we can bust these clowns!" Tracy and Futura leaned closer to hear what he was saying and nodded, while Eddie's uniform began to do a strange dance, its arms and legs waving in the air.

"All right, Kong," roared Prime Evil, "you shall be the first!"

The ghost snakes wrapped themselves around the defenceless Jake and carried him across to Prime Evil. However, just as Prime Evil pushed Jake through the portal, Futura appeared at her full size, and using her powers of telekinesis, floated Jake back into Prime Evil's hands. Immediately, Prime Evil pushed Jake through the portal again and once more Futura did the same.

"Blue-skinned witch!" hissed Prime Evil. "Your powers will tire before my own." Once more, Prime Evil pushed Jake through the portal, and once more Futura brought him back. Suddenly, there was a creaking and groaning and a great splintering of timbers. Tracy, the world's strongest gorilla, had torn apart the treetrunks of the cage where he and Eddie were kept captive. Immediately the ghost snakes attacked the gorilla and the ghostbusting uniform and within moments, had them held tight in their spectral coils. Prime Evil roared with evil laughter and a bolt of lightning sent Futura reeling and somersaulting backwards. "See, Kong!" he roared, picking Jake up once again, "There is nothing that you or your pitiful friends can do to thwart my power!"

Then, as if it was moving on its own, the dematerialiser appeared from one of the ghostpacks, trembled a moment, and then rushed across to Prime Evil and blipped him back across the dimensions. Seeing their master gone, the ghost snakes faded away in fright.

"Nice work, Eddie," said Jake to the trembling dematerialiser.

"Thanks, Jake," said Eddie, handing the

dematerialiser to his partner as first his feet, then his hands, and then his head suddenly reappeared. When his shoulders appeared, Tracy tapped him on them and pointed at his watch.

"I think he's trying to tell you that . . ."

"I know," said Eddie as his hands, head, and feet ran to put on their uniform, "he means that that funny machine he's got with all those squiggly lights inside still isn't working properly."

Later, after the Ghostbusters had won Pibble's confidence with two jelly babies and persuaded him that he'd be much happier riding the ghost train in the ghost zone in the Galaxy of Gribble, Jake was saying goodbye to Chief Charaba when Cornelius Castrol clasped hold of his arm.

"Kong," he said, "I've got it all in the can! Ghosts! Everything!"

"No you haven't," said Jessica. "This is the only camera in the world that takes pictures of ghosts."

"Is that right?" exclaimed Castrol, peering closely at Tracy's invention. "You want to sell it?" Jessica shook her head. Castrol thought for a moment. "Okay, no problem," he said finally. "The guys in special effects can put the ghosts on same time they're putting on the spaceships and the robots and everything else. And you can tell your friend the chief I don't intend filming another foot of film on his tribe's land. As soon as I've got my dinosaurs working . . ."

"Sorry, Mister Castrol, but your dinosaurs are gone," said Eddie. "We gave them to Pibble to play with on his way back to the Ghost Dimension in Gribble."

Waiting For The Witching Hour

As well as a ghostpack full of Ghostbusting gadgets, a successful Ghostbuster needs ingenuity, intelligence, initiative, daring, fortitude, a steady, ice cool nerve, and, most important of all, lashings and lashings of good luck. Of course, it helps if you're just a little bit flakey, too!

You think you fit the description? Then why not take these tests of memory, mental agility, and observation? They're all qualities you're going to need as a Ghostbuster – especially if Eddie's forgotten the plug to the vapour vacuum!?

One more thing. Once you've finished the tests, add up your score and note it down somewhere. It may not seem important, but it is. You'll find out why once you reach The Witching Hour!

TEST NUMBER ONE

Prime Evil's Playthings

These are ghosts and gadgets that you might encounter if you're ever unfortunate enough to have to visit Hauntquarters. All you have to do is fit the right name to each one.

1. Prime Evil's ghostly knight is called: –

   (a) Sir Trancealot
   (b) Sir Goulahad
   (c) Lord Nightmare

2. Prime Evil's control console is called: –

   (a) Ghoulputer
   (b) Computabone
   (c) Bonetroller

3. The name of Prime Evil's intergalactic pirate ghost is:–

   (a) Black Billy Chrome Bones
   (b) Long John Scarechrome
   (c) Long John Hookskull

4. The entrance to Hauntquarters is: –

   (a) The Skullsteps
   (b) The Scarecase
   (c) The Scareway

TEST NUMBER TWO

You are on the Planet Bloop, searching for ghosts. One of the planet's inhabitants has recorded the names of the ghosts you are looking for on a Bloopian communication crystal. You put the crystal into the solar powered cypher unit. However, you have forgotten it is night time and the unit's energy cells are only functioning at half power. These are the names that the cypher unit comes up with.

Can you decipher them?

1. FLATRAZOT 2. ARMY TIES

3. TUN RAT HEHE 4. REAL TRAIN SCOT

TEST NUMBER THREE

Name the following Ghostbusting equipment:

1.

2.

3.

4.

TEST NUMBER FOUR

The powers of observation and memory are important to you, even if you're not a Ghostbuster, so here are four questions from the stories that have been in the book so far. If you can remember the names without looking, score two points for each. If you have to look them up, score only one.

1. What was the name of the talking hat that warned the Ghostbusters that evil was afoot in the faraway world of Gangstonia?
2. What was the name of the truck driver that Prime Evil hypnotised into helping to make his magic potion?
3. Who is the ghost-jailer with the weakness for dreaded wheat and spookhetti sauce?
4. Who was the original owner of the Haunted Pipes of Invermuckly Glen?

ANSWERS

TEST NUMBER ONE 1. (a); 2. (c); 3. (b); 4. (c).
TEST NUMBER TWO 1. Floatzart; 2. Mysteria; 3. The Haunter; 4. Sir Trancealot.
TEST NUMBER THREE 1. Dematerialiser; 2. Ansabone; 3. Skelevision; 4 Ghost Buggy.
TEST NUMBER FOUR 1. Homburg; 2. Meatball Mulligan; 3. Yum-Yum; 4. Drunken Duncan McDiggle.

For days now the crowds had been gathering on the planet Glom. The lobster people from the mining planet of Orebase Seven, the winged octopods of Waterworld, fierce, furry warriors from Cygnus Two, two-headed truckers from the space lanes, spring-powered blobs from the high gravity planets; from all over the galaxy they had come, all with but one thought in mind – to obtain tickets for tonight's Boko concert. For although Boko was only eighteen inches high, he was, in showbiz terms, a giant. In fact, he was the mightiest megastar that the Galaxy of Golum had ever seen. His music crystals sold in their trillions and his songs were relayed by satellite to every inhabited planet, moon, and asteroid in the entire star system. There were Boko t-shirts, life-size Boko holograms and Boko stickers to put on the sides of spaceships. Now, under the interlocking geometric moons of Glom, Boko and his band were performing live.

The crowd were delirious with excitement as the three octopod drummers beat out wild rhythms on their hollow, snailshell drums, their flailing tentacles lashing the water in their tanks to foam. A space walrus plucked out harmonies on his whiskers whilst the wind section raised hairy nose trumpets in the air and sneezed out chorus after chorus with split second timing. And above the hooves and claws, tentacles, trunks, and antennae of the dancing crowd, flew the tiny figure of Boko on his jet trapeze, squeaking and bleeping and buzzing out his wordless songs.

Then, in what seemed an astonishing finale to the Boko Show, a huge, ghostly, glowing building appeared and floated downward from the deep red sky. Strange mists swirled around the building's towers and bats and winged reptiles flew in and out of its windows. From the dripping, moss covered stones emerged a moving staircase, and down it, his coat tails waving like serpents, the tips of his grey moustache trembling with evil anticipation, came a human figure holding aloft a conductor's baton.

Thinking it part of the act, the crowd gasped and filled the air with the sounds of their applause, little realising that the figure was none other than Floatzart, maestro of musical malice. Floatzart gave a sudden flick of his baton and fingers and immediately Boko and his band were silenced, the pounding rhythms of their latest trans-galactic smash replaced by the haunted, hypnotic scales of a magic minuet.

Unable to resist the ghostly music's spell, Boko steered his jet trapeze to the foot of the staircase and stepped onto it. Clouds began to billow overhead, thunder boomed, jagged fingers of lightning stabbed at the spires, and Boko was whisked up into the building as it floated free of the ground and disappeared.

Seconds later, the tiny megastar from the Galaxy of Golum found himself tumbling through tunnels lined with writhing snakes and howling stone heads. Sometimes he fell downwards, sometimes sideways, and sometimes he even seemed to fall upwards. A huge, wooden door creaked open ahead of him and the tiny, purple-eyed star stumbled into a dank, cobwebby dungeon. Clanking chains snaked out from the walls and manacles snapped around his skinny wrists as the door slammed shut behind him.

"I bid you welcome to Hauntquarters, dear Boko," boomed a voice behind him and Boko looked up. There, his eyes glowing brightly through the shadows that surrounded his metal head, was Prime Evil. At his shoulder hovered the malevolent, winged bat-maggot, Brat-a-Rat. "I hope you find the accommodation horrible enough."

"Who ... who ... who are you?" demanded Boko in a trembling squeak as he drew himself up to his full eighteen inches. "A-a-a-and wh-what do you want? A--a-a-a-and why are we, where are we going?"

"Sssssssssilence, pipssssqueak!" hissed Brat-a-Rat, fluttering from Prime Evil's shoulder and sticking his ugly snout out towards Boko. "You are here because the master wishes you to sssssing."

"Indeed I do," crooned Prime Evil, "for horrible though I find the sound of your voice I have discovered that its wavelength and pitch are perfect for my plan. It is a simple matter of sonic polarities. Its vibrations are such that it will de-stabilise the fabric of the transdimensional flux gates and let loose a chaos of ghosts and ghouls upon Earth."

"What's Earth?" asked Boko.

"A mere insignificant speck in space," said Prime Evil. "A place whose future need not concern you. All you have to do is sing one of your horrible songs when we get there and you will be returned safely to Glom."

"And what if I don't?" asked Boko bravely.

"Then you shall stay chained up here forever," hissed Brat-a-Rat, "with the spiders and the rats and the poisonous snakes and the scorpions. And every time midnight strikes I shall come down here and make you take a bath in cold porridge while I whisper stories in your little green ears. Stories so scary that your purple eyes will pop out of your little bald head. And every time that they do, I shall play marbles with them."

"Well, Boko," boomed Prime Evil, "will you help us? You have until midnight to decide."

"When's midnight?" asked Boko nervously.

"It's ALWAYS midnight in Hauntquarters," cackled Brat-a-Rat, wriggling his fat tail round till it pressed a button in the wall. A stone slid back and from behind it rolled out a bath of cold, mildewed porridge. "And midnight means it's bathtime, Boko!"

At 13 Canterbury Street, the Ghostbusters had an emergency on their hands. It had started with the Ghostbusters sitting down to watch a soccer game from the world cup finals in Mexico. Belfry had been eating Brazil nuts that the Ghostbusters had brought back from a Ghostbusting trip to the Amazon rain forest. The crunch and crackle of the shells between the little bat's teeth had been more than Tracy could bear and he had tried to hide the nuts in the Dead Letter File. The file, however, had been in a bad mood and trapped Tracy's fingers in its top drawer and refused to let go. The other Ghostbusters had tugged the gorilla free but they had fallen back over the desk and landed on Skelevision's channel changer bone. They'd either bust it or hurt Skelevision's feelings. Either way, all the skeletal telly would show them were whirling patterns of colour, and now there were only two minutes until the game kicked off.

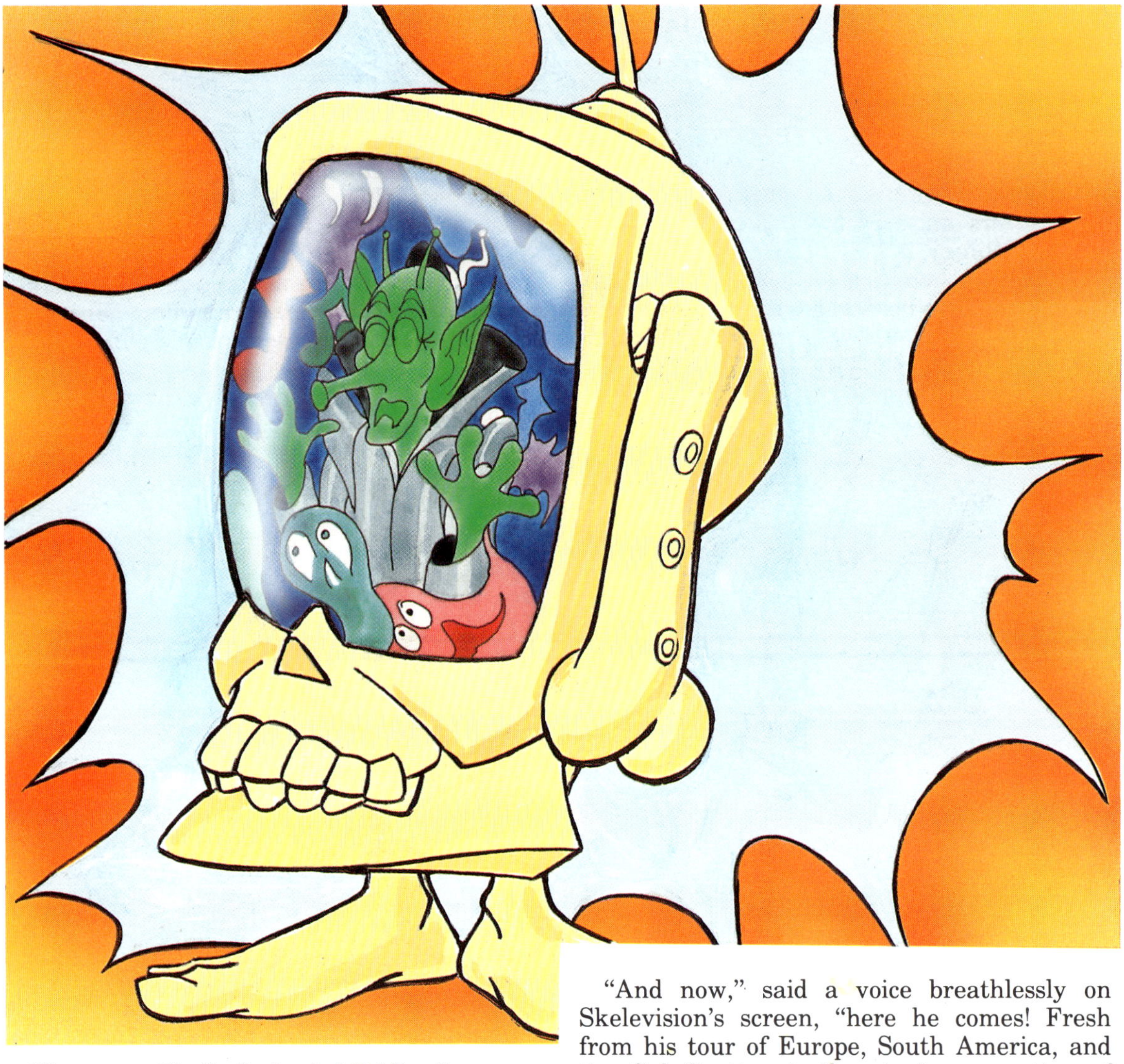

"Come on, Skelly," pleaded Eddie, "you can do it. Show us the soccer."

"You guys are supposed to be Ghostbusters, not sports fans!" snarled Skelevision. "You want to watch something, then watch this."

Suddenly, Skelevision's eyescreen went black, leaving only a tiny dot in its centre. The Ghostbusters groaned in dismay and Tracy had just sprung grimly to his prehensile feet to give Skelevision a good, solid, channel changing slap on top of his skull when the dot grew larger. Eddie said he thought it was a luminous lemon and then the dot grew larger still and the Ghostbusters realised that it was an aerial view of a floodlit stadium. But it was a baseball stadium and there was no game in progress for the field was packed with people. Tracy reached out a finger towards the volume tooth and Skelevision snapped at it and turned up his sound himself.

"And now," said a voice breathlessly on Skelevision's screen, "here he comes! Fresh from his tour of Europe, South America, and the Sub-Continent, the singing sensation of the decade. All the way from Jersey City, the rock and roller who was born to toddle, it's Bruce Wildebeest!"

Saxophones blared, tom-toms pounded, electric guitars echoed around the arena and the huge red curtains that draped the stage slowly opened. But as they did so they revealed not Bruce Wildebeest, the most popular rock and roll singer on Earth, but a strange, silver creature only eighteen inches high. The creature had bulbous purple eyes, a smooth, hairless head, and pointed green ears. Its legs were short and squat, its arms long and spindly, and it began to make furious beeping, buzzing, and squeaking sounds, and with each fresh noise that the creature uttered, strange, spectral shapes began to appear until the entire stadium was a seething, multicoloured mass of ghosts!

"I think we can forget the football, guys," said Jake, "we've got work to do."

With that, the Ghostbusters stepped onto their transportation pads, linked arms, and yelled "Let's go, Ghostbusters!" Immediately the captive ghosts and spectres of Ghost Command came wailing from their hiding places, and with the air in the office full of colour and cacophonous sound, the three Ghostbusters and Belfry dropped down into the Ghost Buggy.

"G.B.," said Jake to the Ghost Buggy as the car spluttered and creaked out into the street, "take us to the baseball ground. You and Belfry are going to be stars!"

"Then you better start changing my oil more often," complained G.B. as the Ghostbusters went to work, pulling drums of cable, old phonographs, bananas, phasers, mayonnaise, catalytic convertors, and the spare parts to a particle accelerator from their ghostpacks. By the time that G.B. swooped down around the Goodyear Blimp to the stadium, Belfry was wired for sound.

"You really want me to go down there?" asked G.B., his radiator coughing nervously. Below them, the huge crowd seemed to bubble and boil like a magic potion in a cauldron. Their faces had changed to the faces of drooling vampires, snarling werewolves and grinning skulls, while above them, in a swirling, transparent mist of blues, greens, greys and reds and strange, freckly, speckly colours that didn't have names, floated thousands and thousands of ghosts.

"You got it, G.B.," yelled Jake. "Let's bust these clowns!"

Immediately, G.B. swooped down among the ghosts, his seats shooting up on springs to allow Jake, Eddie, and Tracy to blip them with the plasm blaster, blop them with the spectral scrambler, and then bloop them back across the dimensions with the dematerialiser. As they approached the stage at the far end of the arena they saw the tiny silver figure of Boko and behind him, his cape swirling, his head a huge silhouette, was the figure of Prime Evil. When the despot saw the Ghostbusters approaching he roared with rage and urged Boko to sing louder still, but as the megastar from the Galaxy of Golum opened his mouth wider, Tracy thrust a banana and mayonnaise sandwich into it and then swung between the scaffolding and giant speakers, trailing lengths of wire and cable behind him, his fingers and toes deftly swapping over plugs and fuses as he went.

"Okay, Belfry," yelled Jake, "give it all you've got!" The little bat leaned into an old phonograph trumpet and his tiny lungs filled up with air and he gave the loudest, longest sonic screech he had ever given in his life. The sound was amplified, accelerated, ionised, phased, dubbed and doctored through the Ghostbusters' sound system, and as it emerged from the huge banks of speakers, the entire stadium began to vibrate. Everywhere ghosts were popping like bubbles and disappearing and werewolves, vampires, and skeletons were suddenly becoming ordinary people once more.

As Prime Evil reached out a claw to grasp Boko, Jake leaned over and clipped the end of his long fingernails with the dematerialiser. Prime Evil gave a shriek of alarm and disappeared up into the sky like a bolt of lightning going backwards. Belfry gave a final, shrill squeak as his lungs ran out of air and the speakers crumbled to piles of black dust, and the audience, looking around at one another and blinking in surprise, began to applaud wildly.

"Scrunchop chebble nurg," said Boko through a mouthful of banana and mayonnaise as Jake tuned in the alien language decoder.

"He says thanks for rescuing him," said Jake, once the decoder was tuned in, "and that if Belfry wants to go back to Golum with him he could make him a star. And he says that the sandwich was delicious."

"Never mind that," said Eddie, "ask if he knows who won the South Korea game."

THE WITCHING HOUR

Jessica Wray has been kidnapped by Prime Evil while investigating strange happenings in a haunted supermarket. In an attempt to lure the Ghostbusters into his clinging, malicious web of evil, the master of misrule has taken Hauntquarters and Jessica to the deepest, darkest, most desolate areas of the Ghost Dimension, far beyond space and time. To get there you will need three Ghostbusting gadgets, two magical objects, one from the future and one from the past, two of your enemies' weapons, and a lump of blutonium superputty to blow in the lock of the spectral dungeon.

Here is how you play. First, get a dice and some counters. Second, check your scores from the tests on pages 51 and 52. If you scored more than sixteen then you start at one o'clock on the Earth Clock. This means that you can immediately pick up the spectral scrambler. If you scored 13–16 start at two o'clock. If you scored 10–12, start at three o'clock. If you scored less than 10 points start at four o'clock – right in the middle of one of Prime Evil's earthquakes.

Now you have discovered your starting points the game can commence.

THE EARTH CLOCK. Throw the dice and move forward, clockwise, the number on the dice. You must collect the Ghost Buggy, the dematerialiser, and the

spectral scrambler. You collect these objects by landing on their square. You must obey whatever instructions there are on the square on which you land. If you have not managed to collect all three gadgets before passing midnight – the witching hour – then you must go round again. As soon as you have collected all three objects you move further inward to the TIME DIMENSION, moving from the square you are on to the one next to it in the new dimension.

TIME DIMENSION. Now you can move freely through time in your quest for Merlin's wand and Futura's amulet. Each square is a different date and you must obey the instructions on each one. You throw the dice to move, but now, although you MUST move, you can move either forward or back. Once you have collected both objects you move inward to the GHOST DIMENSION.

GHOST DIMENSION. Once more you must move the number of dots on the dice. Also, you are able to move in either direction. But watch out, this is a dimension crowded with ghosts and there are many more dangers than before. Once you have collected Apparitia's magic ball, Foatzart's baton, and the blob of blutonium superputty, you must reach the witching hour, for only then does the Scareway to Hauntquarters open long enough to enable you to get inside and rescue Jessica.

If you are playing the game with friends then the winner is the first person to reach Hauntquarters. If you are playing alone, set yourself a time limit and see if you rescue Jessica within that limit.